1

NUTS!
The Life & Times of
General Tony McAuliffe

By

Tom Patrick McAuliffe

NEXT STOP PARADISE
PUBLISHING
Ft. Walton Beach, Florida USA

Nuts!
The Life & Times of General Tony McAuliffe
Copyright © 2022 - All rights reserved.

Any references to historical events, real people, or real places are factual to the best of the authors memory, research and public records.

Second Edition - FALL 2022

For more information email:
bookinfo@nextstopparadise.com

Please leave us a Review!

WWW.AUTHORTOMMCAULIFFE.COM

Nuts!
The Life & Times of General Tony McAuliffe

<u>TABLE OF CONTENTS</u>

Dedication

To my wife Sharon and to my Dad Robert, my Brother Matt and my Brother-in-law Chris and all the brave Veterans who have defended our freedoms through the years.

And to my friend and Cousin Ken McAuliffe, a true American patriot and the Nephew of General McAuliffe, without whom this book would not have been possible.

PREFACE

There have been more books written about World War II than perhaps any other subject short of God. Most provide either an exact moment-by-moment chronological account of the battles or a semi-fictional approach... this volume hopes to be both. It builds on Ken McAuliffe's (the General's nephew) now out of print book and features first-hand interviews with veterans, info from the General's papers, interviews as well as the many other books and documents examining the battles. I hope I have woven together an engaging picture of a remarkable man, my distant relative, his career and the brave soldiers, paratroopers and tankers under his command who, together, gallantly held off Germany's last major offensive and helped America and the Allies to win the war.

I was way too young being born in the 1950s but my Dad served in "The Big One!" as a US Navy Seabee in the Pacific and we talked about the war all the time when I was growing up. As a kid of 9 or 10, perhaps like you, one of our favorite pastimes was 'war games'. In my history classes in High School and College WW II was a subject I always enjoyed exploring. The siege of Bastogne has been documented many times over the past 75 years. One of my first recollections was seeing the 1965 film "Battle of the Bulge" with Henry Fonda and Telly Savalas at the age of 10. The General is also mentioned in the academy award winning movie 'Patton' with George C Scott.

I've always been proud to be part of the McAuliffe clan. General Anthony 'Tony' McAuliffe (1898–1975) was truly one of a kind. He was the epitome of the World War II soldier both cocky and self-assured yet cautious and courteous. He was known for his great sense of humor which endeared him to his men, however he was also known to have a quick Irish temper and no tolerance for BS. The usual consensus was, 'One moment he'd be chewing you out and the next he'd be inviting you to have a beer at the O-club!' McAuliffe was the quintessential American soldier; dedicated, and driven to achieve victory over the Nazis no matter what the cost.

This is the story of his 35+ year career in the US Army and the essential battles, both in person and figuratively, that helped to define it. His many other interesting accomplishments were varied as were his many duty stations. For example he:

•Mastered Artillery and Air Assault Warfare.
• Served in Europe and the Far East Theaters.
• Helped invent numerous military weapons and tools.
• Helped test the atomic bomb.
• Assisted in developing Chemical Warfare Protocol. And lots more during his many years of active duty service. But it was his time spent defending Bastogne, Belgium, during the famous 'Battle of the Bulge' in World War II that is perhaps the most well known.

As temporary Commander of the US Army's 101st Airborne Division (he was always their Artillery Commander), during the siege he's known for his one-word reply when the Germans demanded he and his men surrender. Culled from hundreds of battle accounts, official documents and interviews throughout the years, 'Nuts!' tells the story of McAuliffe and the men he commanded, who overcame being on the road to annihilation in a historic 17th century European City. This is the gritty story of that fateful week in December 1944 when the very outcome of the war lay in the balance. We'd be speaking German if they failed. One wonders if the current generations would step to the plate in similar circumstances today. But this is not a book just about the siege or the Battle of the Bulge or even the War... it is about a man and his intriguing career dedicated to defending America.

I have endeavored to be as accurate as possible which has been a challenge as more and more of these brave men and women pass on. They won the war with determination, luck and good humor and it is vital that America documents and preserves these veterans' stories. I hope Ken and I have done the memory of the General and his men the justice and honor they deserve... we are in their debt forever. They are truly... *The Greatest Generation*'!

Tom
Summer 2022

FORWARD

As the fall of 1944 came to the Ardennes, a 30,000 Square mile forest area of Belgium, the 101st Airborne of the US Army began to settle in for what was supposed to be a calm and quiet R&R time for the troops. It was not to be. As the Nazi's made a last gasp for victory in late fall they broke thru 180 miles of the front with the allies and encircled the town of Bastogne, a central transportation crossroads. Their heroic struggle and their leader, General Anthony McAuliffe, are the subject of this book by his distant relative Tom McAuliffe. Using information from my out of print book, *Nuts-The Life of Anthony C McAuliffe*, many other sources, the author has concentrated on the General's life, career and his famous stubborn response to the German demand to surrender.

What made these guys special? Their willingness to self-sacrifice and their patriotic support for the war effort made these men the 'greatest generation'. From all walks of life they came in the defense of liberty and freedom. So, 80 years on in the troubling times of today where it appears history is indeed repeating itself, it's important that we remember and document what these patriots did so long ago. This is both for our own edification but also to honor and document their sacrifices. The Battle of the Bulge and the siege of Bastogne were perhaps the most critical battles of WWII and it was the good-humored General McAuliffe who led them to victory despite overwhelming odds. It was not unusual that General McAuliffe's first comment after the German's surrender demand was "Nuts". Instead of a swear word like many, Nuts was a non-profane term he used regularly to indicate his disagreement.

In December, 1944 my family was living in Claymont, Delaware where gathering in the breakfast nook each morning and discussing the news of the day became a tradition. On a morning late in December 1944, my Father, General McAuliffe's brother, mentioned that the newspaper had an article that a US Army unit was surrounded in Bastogne, Belgium and that the commanding general had responded "Nuts" to a German surrender demand. On that date, the Army had not yet released which Army unit was surrounded or who the commanding general was.

My Mother immediately said, "That has to be Tony. He always uses that term!" She phoned the General's wife, Helen, who was living in Washington, DC. After a short conversation, they agreed that the "General" in question had to be him! About two days later, the US Army released that the unit was indeed the 101st Airborne Division and that it was Tony.

A great overview of this remarkable man and the men he led to victory, *'Nuts!-The Life & Times of General Tony McAuliffe'* is a wonderful read for any student of Courage, WWII and the famous McAuliffe family.

Kenneth J. McAuliffe Jr.
General McAuliffe's Nephew

CHAPTER 1

Humble Beginnings

"I'm gregarious and I like to be with people."
Tony McAuliffe

On July 2, 1898, Anthony Clemmet McAuliffe was born in the city of Washington, District of Columbia. At the turn of the century, he went through childhood much like any other youngster in middle America.

His parents, John Joseph McAuliffe and Alice Katherine Gannon McAuliffe, went on to have five more children after he was born. His brothers were John, always known as Jack, Kenneth and Richard. Eleanor and Alice were his sisters.

He was born in the Southeast corner of the District, at home. When he was five years old, his family relocated to a neighborhood close by called C. Street. They stayed there until 1921, when his parents made another move this time to Lamont Street, where they spent the remainder of their lives.

"We spent our childhood in a very nice house with hardwood floors and a room that we referred to as the 'Parlor' back in those days. The Parlor was a room with a large crystal chandelier, but it was only utilized when really important guests were in town. The space immediately adjacent to it housed a sizable Library that was furnished with a colossal table and 100s of books," he said. "My dad was an avid reader, and he instilled that love of reading in all of us. He possessed all the classic books, such as those written by Dickens, Thackery, and Fenimore Cooper, as well as poetry and other such things. When we were too small to read on our own, dad would read to us. After that, he encouraged all of us to read, and we have all continued to do so ever since," he recounted. "There was also a dining room beyond that, as well as a wide two-story porch, with three bedrooms on the second level and two on the third floor. All six of us children slept outside on the porch during the summer as well as the winter of our own free will."

Anthony, who would eventually be known as "Tony," was playing sports throughout elementary school and high school, and he particularly liked playing Baseball and Football. On the athletic fields, he excelled not only as a player but also as a natural leader.

"I was born in DC. My father worked at The Interstate Commerce Commission for many years," Tony explains. "He was a master stenographer, and after rheumatoid arthritis disabled his right hand, he became the Manager of the Stenographic Division of the Interstate Commerce Commission." "I was the oldest of six children; there were four boys and two girls in my family, and we all attended public schools."

In terms of size, he was not a very large man and stood approximately 5 feet, 8 inches tall and weighed less than 250 pounds. He exhibited a trim and fit appearance at all times. When he went to family gatherings, he was never referred to as 'General McAuliffe' rather, he was always just "Uncle Tony." He didn't carry himself with any airs and was great at putting people at ease. Tony was also a very sophisticated child for his age, and he spent much of his childhood interacting with either adults or his older siblings. Later in life, people who spent time with him never learned about his many achievements or the famous people he had befriended. That was just not his humble way.

While Tony was a student at the Towers School and Eastern High School, he also developed a strong interest in the military. As a result of this interest, he joined the Washington Cadet Corps, which is a paramilitary club that helps young men and women prepare for careers in the armed forces. He received his diploma from Eastern High School in June of 1916 and expressed interest in enrolling at the United States Military Academy at West Point.

"While I was in the Washington High School Cadets, I had seen some West Point graduates around Washington, and I had seen the them march in the Inaugural and other parades, and I knew the academy's academics were very good, so this was a fine opportunity to get a great education without cost to my father!" he said. At the time, the District of Columbia did not have any Representatives serving in Congress, thus academy applicants had to take a test in order to be considered for an appointment. Tony did not really want to take the test because he believed that he ought to be able to acquire a Congressional appointment based on the good grades he received in high school. After that, all he would need to do is pass a physical examination.

In the interim, as part of his plan, he enrolled at West Virginia University in 1916 and continued his studies there through 1917. During his tenure there, he was also an active participant in the Sigma Phi Epsilon Fraternity.

"After I received my diploma from high school, I was on my way to West Point. After spending a year at the University of West Virginia and establishing a residency there, I was recommended for appointment to West Point from the state of West Virginia," he explained. "I went to West Virginia in 1916, and then on to West Point in June of 1917," he said.

In life, hindsight is always twenty-twenty, but to get a real sense of the man, probably the finest characterization of McAuliffe came years later from his buddy and brother-in-arms, US Army 3-Star General Harry W. O. Kinnard.

Both were members of the 101st at Bastogne, and they remained close friends until each of them passed away. Kinnard, later helped invent 'Air Mobile' warfare in Viet Nam. In the early 1990s

Nephew Ken McAuliffe was given a copy of a letter
that General Kinnard had written about what it was
like to work directly with him. Regarding McAuliffe
as a man, General Kinnard wrote...

"Working with General Tony McAuliffe was a great
pleasure for a number of reasons. First, he was a true
Christian gentleman who was always courteous and
he was always careful to treat people as they should
be treated...which is to say, as he would want to be
treated," Kinnard explained. "Second, he was a very
human and unpretentious man. He had a great sense
of humor and a real gift for making people feel at
ease. I can recall many nights in combat (in
Holland) when he and I, and Paul Danahy (our
Division G-2) and others, would have wonderful
games of Cribbage in the Mess Tent after supper."
Kinard continued, "Third, he was a man who knew

how to fully utilize his staff and elicit their very best efforts. He did this primarily by making it very clear that he had great faith in us and relied on us. Fourth, I always appreciated the fact that, as an Artilleryman, he made no bones about his need to heavily rely on people such as General Gerry Higgins and I (we're both Infantrymen) for advice and counsel regarding aspects of Army operations involving infantry tactics and techniques. This was also true as to questions involving parachuting and parachutists, since General McAuliffe was a Gliderman," he said. "Finally, Tony had a certain avuncular amiable quality which stemmed primarily from his being quite a bit older than his very young staff (for example, I was a full Colonel at only 29 years old). He even hung the title of "Old Crock" on himself as a nickname. His extra years, experience and maturity had a good, steadying influence on all of us," Kinnard concluded.

The passage of time brought about another significant event in McAuliffe's young life and on April 5, 1919, he announced his engagement to the woman who would go on to become his wife, Miss Helen Willet Whitman (1897–1983). She eventually became a frequent visitor to West Point, and Tony never forgot the anniversary date of their first date.

In 1920, he completed his studies at Field Artillery Basic School and received his diploma. The United States Army trains young troops to shoot projectiles in a straight line for a long distance at a high rate of speed at one of the most challenging schools it has.

Tony had no doubt that the requirements of the Army would always come first, but once his training was through, he hoped that he might be stationed in Fort Bragg, North Carolina, so that he could be closer to DC, his family, and his soon-to-be fiancee. However, the Army came to the conclusion that he  would be required at Fort Lewis, which is located in the state of Washington. As a result, the young couple decided to move up their wedding plans, and they tied the knot on August 23, 1920, in front of the bride's loving family and friends, in a ceremony that took place in the bride's home. They were very much in love.

Tony and Helen had their hands full raising a joyful family as Tony started to establish his career in the military. They were blessed with three children:

Patricia Ann (1921-2001), John Hillary, who was always called Jack (1923-1979), and the youngest, Sally Ann (1927-1928), who passed away in her first year, an occurrence that, at the time, was fairly common. Patricia Ann passed away in 2001. John Hillary passed away in 1979.

It was a life straight out of a Norman Rockwell painting, and the family, like most others in the military, spent a lot of time moving from duty station to duty station. The children, Patricia and Jack, accompanied their parents on their travels to Tony's army duties until World War II brought a new level of urgency to the situation. In 1943, when Tony was sent to England to participate in the battle there, his family went back to their origins and re-established their house in Washington, DC.

In 1943, Jack, the General's son, made an application to attend West Point, but he was not successful in receiving an appointment. In 1944, he refused to make use of his father's pull and influence to acquire access to West Point; so instead, he enrolled in the Army on his own. Son Jack received his diploma from the Armored Officer Candidate School at Fort Knox, Kentucky, in July 1945, and father Tony couldn't have been more pleased. Jack was medically retired in 1949 due to a persistent disability. After receiving his degree from George Washington University in 1952, he worked in the state of California until 1966. After, he moved back to DC, and remained there until his death in 1979.

Helen, Patricia, and Jack are all laid to rest in the same section of Arlington National Cemetery as General McAuliffe. This particular section of the cemetery is known as Section 3. Tony, Helen, and Patricia are all going to be laid to rest in the same grave. Due to Jack's service in the Army, he is interred in a separate grave located nearby.

All and all McAuliffe grew up happy, healthy and ready to take on life. He was taught a deep love of America and came to believe that it was his duty to defend it. He didn't know it at the time but he would get his chance.

CHAPTER 2

"Stand At Attention!"

"When the patriotic bullshit is all said and done you ask yourself... Do I trust these guys with my life? And in the finale of battle sometimes in the end the answer was no, if yes... one should be prepared to hold their best friends head in their lap watching them gasp their last breath."
US Army Solider, WWII

McAuliffe joined the United States Army's "long gray line" in 1917 at The United States Military Academy at West Point. He participated in an expedited officer program and graduated not long after the end of World War I, in November 1918. McAuliffe graduated from the rapid officer program. Tony was nominated as an alternative for an appointment to West Point by Congressman Neely of the 1st District of West Virginia. With the assistance of his Great Uncle, Reverend Patrick James Donahue, who was the Bishop of Wheeling, West Virginia, Tony was able to get this nomination. Tony was given the chance to qualify since the person who was supposed to fill the position did not pass the physical exam. The one thing that worried Tony most about the real physical was the weight requirement, which needed him to be at least 117 pounds. Tony was thin and barely weighed 114 pounds when he went in for his medical on the morning of the exam! To reach the target weight, he gorged himself on bananas and guzzled down gallons of water. He had to wait for quite some time, but in the end, it was all worth it and he got accepted.

"The course at West Point is designed to build a person's character and to fulfill the motto of the Academy, which is 'Duty! Honor! Country!' I think the greatest thing that's accomplished at West Point is instilling in its graduates this motto and those attributes which will make the solider live up to it and thus become a dedicated and effective leader," McAuliffe said. "My ambition was to command troops in battle, and I feel that's the ambition of most military people. If you specialize, you get sidetracked, so I tried to be as generic as possible in regard to military specialities," he said. At West Point, "I was in the 'first section'. Your graduation status is based on your grade point average, with the first section having the highest average grade. I was placed in the top class in most courses, notably mathematics, and my teacher there was a gentleman by the name of Timothy. Timothy had graduated from West Point three classes after I had done so. He was the top student in his high school and went on to have a successful career as an engineer and eventually rose to the rank of Major General. He was an excellent and capable instructor, and taught me well," the General recalled. "Since I was not one of the better students, I was sent down to the second section when we started doing descriptive Geometry. I did so poorly in the first part. After we finished, I went back and started taking Calculus classes again and did well so I was allowed to move back into the first section," he said.

The Cadets did not have a lot of things to divert their attention away from the tasks at hand. "Each man at West Point has an alcove, a locker, and a place to store his rifle, as well as a table and chair where he studies. The rooms at West Point are pretty standard and sparse; every morning you fold back your mattress and pile your bedding neatly on top of it and that's it!" he added. "They are really strict regarding cleaning and making sure that your brass is polished and your linens are clean, etc. When I first arrived at West Point, I was pretty careful and

interested in my personal hygiene, and I rapidly learned how to improve all aspects of life throughout my time there."

Young McAuliffe went through a period of self-discovery and personal development at this time. The Academy, which was established two centuries ago on the oldest Army base in the nation provides instruction in 37 distinct fields of study. Its primary focus is developing students' character and military bearing. McAuliffe had the code, which states that,

"A Cadet will not lie, cheat, or steal nor tolerate those who do!" drilled into his head and heart, and he carried those principles with him until the day he died. But in addition to this, he was fully aware, that despite the fact that one may eventually get a college degree for one's efforts, all this was really about going to war, and that someone was going to get shot!

"I believe that every student who enrolls at West Point harbors the secret hope that one day they will be in a position to direct combat operations involving American armed forces, and I was no exception," he said. "I suppose a part of me wished that I would be given that chance," he said. "But when you're studying History and Algebra it can be difficult to keep in mind that one may have to kill one's enemy."

Tony was eager to launch a successful Army career and earn a good reputation as quickly as possible. "I had been informed that they were suffering from a severe lack of Lieutenants in the Infantry in Europe for the duration of World War I, and that as a result, they desired to commission us and send us over there as soon as possible to begin fighting. But on the 11th of November, only ten days after we graduated, the WW1 came to an end, and an armistice was signed. At that point, they dispatched the entire class back to West Point," he said. "Our time at West Point was quite brief, yet during that time we graduated a number of really talented men."

In 1920, he received his diploma from the Artillery School of the United States Army and was subsequently assigned to the Military Occupational Specialty (MOS) of Field Artillery (MOS 0844). Then McAuliffe served in conventional peacetime

 assignments throughout the next sixteen years of his career. It was not because of poor performance that advancement came slowly; rather, it was because of an increase in the number of officers in the Army as a result of World War I. "If you can believe it, I served as a Lieutenant for the better part of 17 years. I served as a Lieutenant for approximately the same number of years as I did as a General!" McAuliffe said. By 1935, Tony had already achieved the rank of Captain. After that, he was given the opportunity to study at the United States Army Command and General Staff College, which is located at Fort Leavenworth. In June of 1940, McAuliffe completed his studies at the War College and received his diploma.

Just a few short weeks before the surprise attack on Pearl Harbor in December 1941, McAuliffe received another promotion, this time to the rank of Lieutenant Colonel in the Supply Division of the War Department. McAuliffe was determined... He had a task to do, and come hell or high water, he was

going to get it done. This is not to say that he was arrogant or boastful in any manner; rather, he was just confident in the knowledge that he would somehow succeed. But there was no room for error in his scenario. It was evident to him that some were headed for a body bag but you just knew that other guys were not going to get even a scratch. To him some guys run... some remain... some surrender... some fight. He was adamant about getting himself prepared to fulfill his responsibilities. McAuliffe came to the realization that there are two types of leaders: one commands "go do it," and the other says and extols "come on guys let's go do it together." He strived to be the second type of leader.

CHAPTER 3

The Big One: WWII

"If everyone is thinking alike,
someone isn't thinking."
General George S. Patton

No solider wants war. And Tony McAuliffe didn't
either. But he was unafraid and ready to fully utilize
his skills and training to defend his nation
McAuliffe was more than ready and in fact, eager to
put his training and the tools and technologies of
war he had helped to develop the full test. But from
his military experiences to date and from what he
had heard about Nazi atrocities, it was very clear to
McAuliffe that any schoolyard sensibilities would
not survive on the battlefield and that this was not
some sort of advanced science experiment or Boy
Scout camp out.

In 1944, despite the fact that most people in
Germany wanted the war to end, Hitler was not
prepared to concede defeat. So the Germans
launched one final assault in an effort to break
through the Allied lines of defense. On December
16, 1944, the Nazis used the strategy of Blitzkrieg to
cut through the Ardennes Forest. The Allied forces
were taken completely by surprise, and they made
frantic efforts to prevent the Germans from making
their way toward their goal, the port of Antwerp.
Because of this, the Allied line started to have a

bulge in it, which is why the battle was given the name "Battle of the Bulge." It was to be the fiercest battle American forces had ever fought.

After four long years of war, both Allied and Axis soldiers, as well as the population they guarded, were exhausted and drained. The conflict had been going on for four years. By the fall of 1944, the German Reich had caused the death and devastation of millions of people across thousands of kilometers, ranging from the eastern front in Russia to the coast of the Atlantic in France.

By that point, more than 2 million soldiers had been killed, and the Nazi forces had taken control of over 1.7 million square kilometers of land throughout Europe, the middle east, and northern Africa. However, the Luftwaffe (German army) was also exhausted and suffering from a lack of supplies and fuel. The industrial infrastructure of Germany and its capacity to refine oil had been reduced to rubble as a result of the bombing by Allied air forces.

The sound of Nazi gunfire piercing the stillness of Belgium's vast and snow-covered Ardennes woodland provoked widespread terror among military and civilian alike. The majority of the members of the Allied army were either newly arrived soldiers who had just stepped off the ship or veterans who had just returned from the front lines and were worn out, hungry, and cold. Ten armored German divisions, some of which were equipped with the newly improved 'Tiger' Panzer tank, and twenty-five infantry divisions launched an assault on the Allied line that stretched some 500 miles, from Holland to France and the Atlantic Ocean.

As the fall of 1944 progressed, many people felt that Germany and Italy were very close to being defeated and that they did not have much more time left. But by the beginning of December, the Nazis covered 29,500 square miles in Belgium's Ardennes region, causing widespread terror and ultimately leading to massive destruction. The Nazi objective was to break through the American and British lines divide them and sap their will to fight and hopefully destroy their partnership. Adolf Hitler yearned for a repeat of the astounding victories he had experienced in 1940, when he had successfully taken over the very same territory. This time, the surprise German onslaught had produced a massive 'bulge' in the front lines and had encircled the strategic town of Bastogne, which had been a crossroads since the 17th century. As the Germans advance, less than 500 soldiers from the 101st Airborne and the 10th Armored Division are left trapped and isolated in the dead of winter.

The weather had an undeniably significant role, both in terms of the cloudy skies that prevented allied air power from flying forcing them to remain on the ground, as well as the sub-zero temperatures which affected everyone. The winter of '44 was one of the coldest winters in more than 100 hundred years and from frostbite to soldiers having to pee on their guns so they would fire, to the oil in their tanks freezing, the forces on either side were ill-prepared for fighting in such harsh winter conditions and they did not have the appropriate arctic equipment to do so.

The ultimate goal of the Nazis was to eventually negotiate a cease-fire. It turned out to be an illusion. In 1940, Adolf Hitler achieved a tremendous victory in this very same region, and he hoped to achieve a similar result this time around. Hitler was fully aware that the British and American soldiers were stretched thin and that they were not accustomed to combat in such terrible winter conditions. He also knew that the weather would be a factor in their performance. Those who were left surrounded gained the reputation of being known as the "Bastards of Bastogne," which is a play on the phrase "those miserable bastards" and refers to their potential near-term destiny. Hitler was not ready to admit defeat despite the fact that many people in Germany were ready to end World War II, and reports suggested that he never would be. The attempt on the Führer's life the previous summer affected him deeply and had made him more paranoid than usual. He was willing to destroy the world, or at least Europe, rather than admit defeat and do what was best for his people and those left behind.

The Germans attempted to breach the Allied line and sow conflict between the commanders of the United States and the United Kingdom. Their immediate objective was to go all the way to Antwerp and take control of the port as well as the Allied supply base there. In particular, they needed gasoline for their tank engines which, due to the cold, needed to run 24/7. Their ultimate goal was to break up the alliance, get to the negotiating table, and then be able to utilize German soldiers on the eastern front against Russia. They hoped that this would be possible. The deadliest battle ever fought by American forces would take place in an area of fewer than 150 square miles and over the period of less than a month. During the course of the conflict, an unprecedented number of soldiers, assets and supplies would be mobilized.

TANK MAN!

The lovely little hamlet of Bastonge served as the intersection of seven important roadways and was known as 'the crossroads of eastern Belgium' because of its location. Harold Burgess was a Tank Commander for the 4th Armored Division when he joined the 10th Armor Division as a temporary attachment after being separated from his own regiment. Before the Nazis sealed off the entrance to Bastogne, his tank was one of the very last ones to enter the city. As he was making his way to a good firing position to the north of the town, he was met with "some resistance."

"When the attack finally came, I was hunkered down inside my Sherman. The first round was deflected by the armor, but the second one hit on the right side with hot metal shrapnel entering my thumb just above the joint," he said. He never removed the piece of shrapnel from his thumb and

he always joked that he had 'brought home a 'piece of history!' "When we were under assault, I would clench my hands until they were on the verge of breaking and bite the inside of my lip till it bled. The other side was really giving us the business and the boom of a German .88 was so loud that it seemed like someone had body checked you in hockey whenever it rang out. They were able to pound the hell outta us with those!"

Burgess, like the majority of the guys who served under McAuliffe's command, had terrifying tales to tell... "It was a week before Christmas, and I had come out of my tank to take a pee and get some fresh air, even though it was rather chilly outside at minus 7 degrees. It was a full moon, and as a result, the forest road looked almost exactly like it does during the twilight hours. Both the Germans and the men of the 101st were out on patrol. 5 or 6 of our guys were walking near the Tank when all of a sudden, four Krauts popped up out of a fox hole that they had covered with some Pine branches (they were resting up before giving us some business!) And everyone stood perfectly still for perhaps 30 seconds, although it seemed like an hour. Suddenly, both squads began firing, and I dove behind the tank and crawled back inside. The 101st squad incurred three deaths out of seven that night. But that frozen response and the expression in my adversary's eyes are things that I will never forget," he said. After a while, Burgess was able to get back to his unit, where he was given a new tank, finished out the rest of the war, and then returned to his home state of Michigan. •

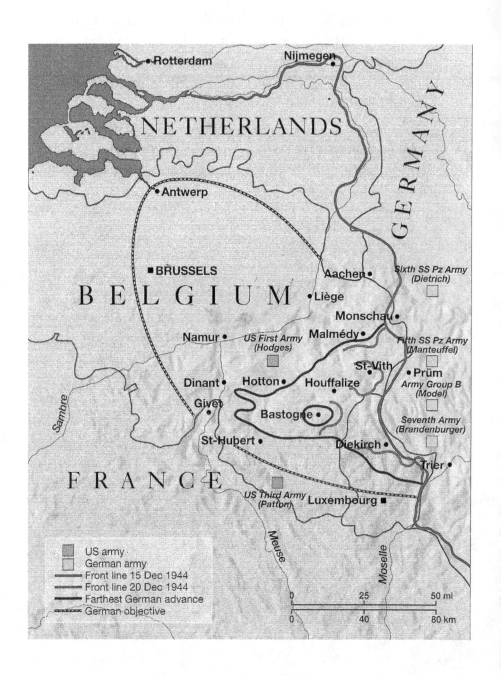

- Rotterdam
- Nijmegen

NETHERLANDS

GERMANY

- Antwerp

■ BRUSSELS

B E L G I U M

- Aachen
- Liège

Sixth SS Pz Army
(Dietrich) □

- Monschau
- Malmédy

Namur •   US First Army
(Hodges) ■

Fifth SS Pz Army
(Manteuffel) □

- St-Vith
- Prüm

Army Group B
(Model)

Dinant •   Hotton •   Houffalize

Givet •

Bastogne •

Seventh Army
(Brandenburger) □

St-Hubert •

Diekirch •

Trier •

F R A N C E

US Third Army
(Patton) ■

Luxembourg ■

Sambre

Meuse

Moselle

□ US army
□ German army
— Front line 15 Dec 1944
— Front line 20 Dec 1944
— Farthest German advance
··· German objective

| 0 | 25 | 50 mi |
| 0 | 40 | 80 km |

CHAPTER 4

Surrounded!

"Men, we are surrounded by the enemy. We have the greatest opportunity ever presented an Army. We can attack in any direction!"
General Tony McAuliffe

Ten German armored divisions sporting the newly improved 'Tiger' Panzer tank (more armor and longer shooting distance), as well as 25 crack infantry divisions launched towards the Allied line that stretched from Holland in the North all the way across to France in the South. Gunfire shattered the silence of the vast fog-shrouded Ardennes forest in Belgium, causing upheaval and terror. Hitler was well aware that the British and American soldiers were stretched thin and were not accustomed to combat in cold winter conditions, and he planned to take advantage of these facts. The surprise German offensive had created a huge 'bulge' in the front lines and had encircled the historic town of Bastogne, which dates back to the 17th century. They became known as the "Bastards of Bastogne," which is a play on the phrase "those poor bastards," which is a remark on the potential that lay ahead.

McAuliffe, age 46 at the time of the battle, recalled how the American Army had prepared well for the type of circumstances that arose in Bastogne, and he also recalled how everything had worked out in the end. "I have no doubt that the two airborne divisions that were established way back in August 1942 were established with the D-Day operation and the possibility of operating behind German lines in mind. The objective of the unit? Mobility!" McAuliffe said,

Following orders, he reported to General William C. Lee at Camp Claiborne, in the state of Louisiana. At the time, General Lee commanded the 101st Airborne Division, which had just been formed.

"In the beginning, it had three infantry regiments and three artillery battalions, as well as an anti-aircraft battalion and an engineering battalion. However, by the time I deployed overseas, all of these things had changed. In point of fact, we had four Infantry Regiments before we were done, and in Bastogne we had extra Artillery Battalions, quite a number of them, including several Marine Corps and Army Artillery Battalions with higher caliber weapons. But, as I've already mentioned, when we first started out, we only had three infantry units," McAuliffe said.

In point of fact, the Army had taken an infantry division known as the 82nd Infantry Division and divided it in half to create the 82nd Airborne (whose motto is "Death From Above") and the 101st Airborne (also known as "The Screaming Eagles")

"We began at Claiborne, but after a relatively short period of time spent training there, we moved to Fort Bragg in North Carolina. Fort Bragg was a very attractive place and a much better place to train because it had sandy soil, was clean, and was large. It also had good artillery ranges and good areas for maneuvering. In addition to that, we were able to acquire some quarters on the post, and I relocated my wife to Fort Bragg in one of the quarters that we had acquired on the post," McAuliffe added. It was indeed all about… 'Death from Above'.

"We continued with this training until 1943, when we finally embarked on our mission to Europe. Now, the 82nd Airborne division had already gone over a little while before we did. They went to North Africa and took part in the invasion of Sicily. During that invasion, there was a mix-up, and the 82nd lost some airplanes and their Assistant Division Commander, Charlie Keerans, who was a close friend of mine, was killed. Both of these tragedies occurred early on in my time there," he said sadly.

"We ultimately advanced to a region immediately south of the Rhine River, where the Germans were located on the opposite bank, and there, we engaged in a significant number of fire fights. It was uncomfortable, freezing... God, it was dreadful. When it thawed, you'd be up to your knees in slush, and when it froze, it was awful. However, despite the weather the Germans continued to be active, and a significant number of mortar and artillery shells were being fired at us all the time."

When McAuliffe and company arrived to the European theater and got settled down, they didn't really expect they'd go anywhere until the spring. "We knew that the crossing of the Rhine was scheduled for that time," he added. "So we didn't think we'd go anywhere. We believed that we had four months to prepare before the Bulge happened, but it turned out that we were wrong."

So the German advance continued. "Colonel Heaton gave me a call. He asked whether or not I was aware that the Germans had launched a surprise offensive in the Ardennes, and after I responded yes, he simply said, "You know where the danger is. You have to get ready and get up there!" So I gathered my staff together, revoked all passes and started to plan," McAuliffe said. But he was shorthanded. During this time, General Ridgway had given permission for General Higgins, Colonel Sink, and a few other officers to travel to England to discuss the airborne operations. "In all honesty, I have no doubt that the true motive was to go to the wedding of

Colonel Dobie, a Britisher who had been a wonderful friend to both of us," McAuliffe recalled.

Every soldier reacts differently to stress, making it impossible to predict when they will cross the line from being in charge to being emotionally overwhelmed. "Before the siege, I used to go over to General Taylor's house for breakfast in the morning. I would eat there with General Higgins, who was the Assistant Division Commander, Colonel Millener, who was the Chief of Staff, and myself. General Taylor would also join us on occasion, but he was currently back in Washington for discussions," McAuliffe said. "Then, all of a sudden, a French servant ran in and broke the news to us that the Colonel was dead! I couldn't believe what I was hearing, so I rushed upstairs to check. To my horror, I saw Millener lying dead on the floor of the bathroom with the barrel of a .45 caliber service revolver stuck in his mouth. It appeared as though he had blasted his brains all over the ceiling of the bathroom, and there was a large pool of blood. The news that Millener had killed himself came as such a shock to me, to everyone... Then I walked into his bedroom, and I saw that he had a work by Tolstoy called "The Brothers Karamazov," which is a really dismal and crazy kind of book, open beside his bed. I don't know, looking back on it, I think I should have guessed it. I had a terrible feeling of shame since I hadn't been able to see what was about to happen, but it turned out that no one else had either." He said.

BASTOGNE
BASTION
OF
THE BATTERED
BASTARDS
OF THE 101ST.

The journey that McAuliffe and his troops were about to go on would go down in the annals of history, and the town of Bastogne would never be the same. "So we continued driving until we reached a junction of roads approximately four kilometers to the west of Bastogne. I was aware that the VIII Corps was present, but my knowledge of the situation was quite limited. As a result, I made the sudden decision to drive into Bastogne and investigate the situation for myself firsthand," McAuliffe explained. "I got in my jeep and drove into town, where I went to visit General Middleton, who was the commander of the VIII Corps. "How did you know to come here?" he said. And I said, "I didn't know anything about anything!" He answered by saying, "You're not going to fight at Werbomont at all. Now you're coming here to defend this town!"

It was impossible to control that region of Belgium without Bastogne. It's located at the intersection of seven major roadways that served as a bottleneck since all of the highways — south, east, west, north, northeast, northwest, and southeast — pass through it, which makes for an ideal location from which to ambush the enemy. "During the course of that night, we discussed what actions we ought to take. As someone who had just arrived on the scene, I, along with General Middleton, was unaware of the current situation" McAuliffe said. "The 501st was the main regiment, and it was now headed by a Colonel named Julian Ewell, West Point class of 1939. What a soldier he was! At the age of 26, he was most likely the youngest leader of a unit during World War II!" he said. "Well, we debated that night about what we should do and after thinking on it for a long while, I still didn't know what to do, so I called Ewell in and I said, "Tell ya what... you take the 501st tomorrow and march out this road, and I want your leading elements to clear this crossroads by six o'clock in the morning; march east, make contact with the Germans, attack, and develop the situation," said General McAuliffe. "So, for a day or so the Germans nursed their wounds, and then they started to move, as I suspected they might, first

around to the north of us. So, I threw the 506th Regiment in on the left of Ewell's regiment, the 501st, and they had quite a firefight and encountered some tanks. And we found when we got there the 10th Armored Division, so we did indeed have tanks, and a battalion of tank destroyers in addition to fine artillery support." So the Germans, as McAuliffe had thought they would, began to move. "After that, I deployed the 506th Regiment to the left of Ewell's 501st Regiment, and they got into a rather intense engagement when they came across several Nazi Panzer tanks. And when we arrived, we discovered that our 10th Armored Division had set already up a Combat Command there. This meant

that we did, in fact, have assets and support." Given what they were up against the Allies needed all the help they could get!

With all the excitement, it appeared as though no one was left to mind the store. When the assault on Bastogne began, the commander of the 101st Airborne Division, Major General Maxwell D. Taylor, was in the United States for a staff meeting. McAuliffe had the responsibility of commanding the 101st and the men that were assigned to it while Taylor was absent. He did so. The Germans, led by General Heinrich Freiherr von Lüttwitz, besieged the town in far greater numbers and force than the Americans.

The events surrounding "Nuts" and the real call for surrender made by the Nazis has been the subject of contrasting interpretations throughout the years. Nephew Ken McAuliffe was able to discern what really took place after conducting a substantial amount of study and having direct conversations with both the General and the men that were present.

The German Commander Von Lüttwitz issued an ultimatum on the 22nd of December, 1944. He sent a negotiating delegation to deliver it under the cover of a flag of truce. The negotiation group consisted of a German Major, a Lieutenant, and two enlisted men. After breaking through the American lines to the southeast of Bastogne, they were taken by Company F to headquarters where the German team handed General McAuliffe's staff the following note:

To the U.S.A. Commander of the encircled town of Bastogne.
The fortune of war is changing. This time the U.S.A. forces in and near Bastogne have been encircled by strong German armored units. More German armored units have crossed the river Ourthe near Ortheuville, have taken Marche and reached St. Hubert by passing through Hompre-Sibret-Tillet. Libramont is in German hands. There is only one possibility to save the encircled U.S.A. troops from total annihilation: that is the honorable surrender of the encircled town. In order to think it over a term of two hours will be granted beginning with the presentation of this note. If this proposal should be rejected one German Artillery Corps and six heavy A.A. Battalions are ready to annihilate the U.S.A. troops in and near Bastogne. The order for firing will be given immediately after this two hours term. All the serious civilian losses caused by this artillery fire would not correspond with the well-known American humanity.
The German Commander

The General continues, "On Tuesday, the 22nd. I returned to my command post, which was located in the basement of the barracks, after paying a visit to the troops, (as the General frequently did since he believed that such visits boosted troop morale). Colonel Harper of the 327th was on duty and he reported that a couple of German officers, along with a soldier with a white flag on a stick, had been blindfolded and taken into his regimental command post," McAuliffe added. "I opened the German's note and it was a call for us to surrender, indicating that the fortunes of war had shifted and informing me what towns were in German hands behind, north and south of us... everywhere!" He said. "They'd given us several blows throughout the night, yet we were still whole after all of it. And it stated that all of the civilian losses would not be in conformity with the infamous American humanity or some corny thing to that effect, which irritated me," he remarked. "And it stated that the most respectable thing I could do in this situation would be to surrender. So I just responded with the word "Nuts," and then continued on with my day. I went out once more to check on some of my soldiers on the western side of the perimeter, and when I returned to HQ after about an hour, Colonel Harper informed me that the German emissaries were still present. They informed us that they had presented a formal official document, therefore they are entitled to a response that is also formal and official. So I invited them to "come on up. We'll hand you one." When I asked the staff members who were around what the appropriate response should be, Kinnard responded by saying, "That first crack of yours would be just the ticket!" So I said, 'Go ahead and write it up.' The German had written "The German Commander" over the signature of his message, which he had sent to "The American Commander in Bastogne." The staff then handed me a piece of paper that had been written with the following message:

"To the German Commander
Nuts!
The Commander of the United States"

I went ahead and signed it, and then Harper walked
over, got the letter, and gave it to the Germans. He
then took off their blindfolds and led them to the
outpost line," McAuliffe stated. "The German
Colonel then said, 'If this reply is favorable, I have
permission to discuss further terms," to which
Harper responded, "the reply is not favorable; it
consists of a single word... Nuts." The German
responded, "Well, I thought I knew English, but I
don't understand 'Nuts' in this context," to which

Harper said, "It means the same as 'Go to hell.' Are you able to understand that?" The Nazi responded with a "Yes, I do." And Harper responded, "On your way, Bud," and that was it. There was no further discussion," he recalled. McAuliffe, in his usual fashion, went with the exclamation "Nuts!" rather than anything more 'down- to-earth' or profane. Captain Vincent Vicari, who was serving at the time as the General's personal aide, remembered that, "General 'Mac' was the only general I've ever known who didn't curse." The term "nuts" was frequently used in his everyday language and some people, many years later, asserted that NUTS was really an abbreviation for the phrase 'Not Understanding the Terms of Surrender.'

According to McAuliffe, even though it turned out to be a significant development in the long run thru the lens of history, it never truly appeared that way at the time. He stated that they had the impression that they were only engaged in a minor skirmish. "That this caused such a commotion initially and thereafter caught all of us off guard, and it still does. We had the impression that this was only for our own consumption." McAuliffe and his troops were also unaware that their answer and reluctance to surrender, had infuriated Hitler. However, they were aware of the vital role of Bastogne at that time, as McAuliffe explained, "All you had to do was look at the map!"

On the evening of December 25, 1944, Brigadier General Tony McAuliffe and his staff were gathered

DEATH FROM ABOVE!

101st Airborne 'Screaming Eagles'

General Tony McAuliffe talks with his troops before Operation Market Garden and the invasion of the Netherlands in September 1944

inside the Heintz Barracks in Bastogne for Christmas supper. During the course of the siege, these military barracks conducted double duty as the Division Main Command Post and Mess Hall.

Although many infantry and artillery attacks were launched at Allied positions, the anticipated full-on Nazi tank attack did not materialize. However, the Americans were cut off from other troops and could do little but wait for the onslaught. But that wasn't all; on top of that, the German Luftwaffe launched a merciless assault on the town, hitting it nightly with artillery and mortars. The 101st fought off the Germans until the 4th Armored Division arrived on December 26 to provide reinforcements. Following closely behind them was General George Patton and the United States 3rd Army.

"They were forced to drop all of these supplies by parachute to us because we were running so low on ammo in addition to, of course, food and other things. They accomplished this and I believe on Christmas Eve, they were successful in bringing us a large quantity of ammunition, which was desperately needed," McAuliffe recalled. "In the meantime, General Patton had been forced to make a U-turn and was making quick progress northward toward us. I relayed to him that I believed we could maintain our position for almost a week until he and the 3rd Army could reach us and we stood firm for a total of eight days," he said proudly.

"So, on Christmas Day, I was making sure to stay in contact with General Middleton in order to find out exactly where the lead elements of General Patton's 3rd Army was located. I worked up a code with General Middleton to know when they arrived. Then, late Christmas night, I went out to the outpost line and greeted the leading elements of the 4th Armored Division of Patton's Army. They were led by a Captain named Dwight, who was in the battalion of Lt. Colonel Abrams, who is now a Lt. General. As a result, I knew they were close, and on that night, I went out to the line and we found them. There weren't a lot of formalities involved. I merely said, "I sure am glad to see you!" They expressed that they were pleased to see me as well, and then they entered the town. It was a really exciting and dramatic time. Everyone in our group found out at about the same time, but I don't think it was much more of a dramatic occasion than the very next day when Allied airplanes dropped the supplies to us. That was a wonder to see. Everyone was aware that we did not have enough ammo and that we were really very hungry."

The dinner on Christmas Day was special. Special not because it was the holiday and there were 100's of German troops surrounding them; it was because McAuliffe's men had made it special. "We still had some K-rations and other stuff that was canned. We discovered a lot of flour there, so the cook prepared some pancakes. We also found a lot of Cognac, which the VIII Corps had abandoned (and then sought to retrieve), but we did not hand it over to

them," he smiled, "After the hospital was destroyed, we were unable to procure any morphine or other necessary medications for the injured, so we were forced to give them Cognac instead. Several hundred people were injured on our side. Immediately they brought in some surgical teams and volunteers using gliders, and they were incredibly helpful in taking care of the most severely injured of our soldiers," McAuliffe stated.

For his efforts in defending Bastogne, General McAuliffe was awarded the Distinguished Service Cross by Patton while he was still on the battlefield (see back cover). McAuliffe was then warded his second star, elevated to the rank of Major General, and given full command of the 103rd Infantry Division on January 15, 1945, immediately following Bastogne. Because it was his first full division-level command assignment, which he maintained until July 1945, he felt both happy and proud.

"General Taylor arrived and expressed his satisfaction and pride in what all of us had done there. And not long after that, I received a phone call from General Eisenhower's Chief of Staff, General

Bedell Smith, who had been an old friend of mine, and he congratulated me and then told me that I was going to have my very own division, the 103rd Infantry, and he told me that I should get started, immediately, so General Taylor threw a dinner party for me that night with most of the staff. I was very excited about the news and during the party they gave me a pair of canvas leggings to wear as a symbol of the fact that I was transitioning from the position of a Paratrooper to that of an Infantry soldier, and I will never forget that. I was very close to tears!" said McAuliffe.

The following day, Bastogne was already in the rearview mirror, with the General and the 103rd already on their way to Germany and Berlin. In March, the 103rd Infantry Division, which was commanded by McAuliffe, arrived in the Rhine Valley and began engaging in mopping up operations west of the Rhine River. In April of 1945, the division was given a temporary assignment of local policing tasks but they quickly returned to the offensive and started following an enemy retreating across Germany.

On the 27th of April, troops of the division entered Landsberg, which was the location of the Kaufering

Concentration Camp, which was a sub-camp of Dachau. The unspeakable horror that was discovered there has become legendary and what they saw there had a definite effect on McAuliffe and his troops. But they moved rapidly onward and after crossing the Danube River on May 3, 1945, members of the 103rd Infantry Division took control of the city of Innsbruck in Austria with little to no resistance. After that, it took Brenner Pass and proceeded into Italy, where McAuliffe linked up with the 88th Infantry connecting the Italian and Western European fronts. It was quite evident to McAuliffe and everyone else that they were getting closer to the end rather than the beginning. •

The Angels of Bastonge

War is a bloody business regardless of when or where it is taking place, and the Bastogne Nurses were indeed the finest of the best and God's Angels on earth. There is a tale that emerged from the siege of Bastogne that is not widely known. It was rumored that when McAuliffe heard the story in its entirety, he almost broke down in tears.

The Battle of the Bulge was one of the largest and bloodiest battles in American history. After the Germans captured the local military Field Hospital complete with all of its medical equipment, supplies, and staff, the surrounded soldiers in Bastogne had no medical assistance at all. None. When they were

59

shot, they either bled to death in the crimson snow or their fellow troops did what little they could with whatever resources and tools they could find.

In 1944, Bastonge was a freezing nightmare on earth. Enter Dr. Jack Prior, United States Army Medical Corps, 20th Armored Infantry Battalion and the great state of Ohio. In a matter of an hour, he rigged up a makeshift aide station in the cellar of the Sarma General Store on Rue de Neufchateau, a main street in town. In essence, it was just someplace out of the cold. Suddenly two local women appeared out of nowhere to offer assistance.

The Belgian nurse Augusta Chiwy (1921-2015), whose name is not well recognized until around half a century after the siege, was by the Doctor's side day and night. A black lady who was born in the Congo, together with Dr. Prior, she toiled till they were exhausted, bravely rescuing countless lives in the midst of blood, tears, cries, and death. Those who could not be saved had their suffering minimized as much as was humanly possible. Chiwy learned her talents as a healer all on her own, and

 she did not become a Registered Nurse until well after the war. At one point, Chiwy put on a

uniform from the United States Army in order to go out into the field and gather wounded soldiers while they were under attack. An accomplishment that has not yet been appropriately recognized and rewarded in full. According to this author's point of view, she ought to be honored with a medal. In the improvised "Hospital," there was dust and dampness everywhere, and the air smelled simply like... death. They worked together to save as many people as they could with the resources they had. Sheets were used as bandages, bottles were inverted and transformed into IV's, boards were fashioned into splints, and the only anesthetic available at all was French Wine or Cognac.

Chiwy collaborated with a second volunteer, a beautiful young local nurse by the name of Renee Lemaire. She had previously had a position at the nearby hospital before the war. In December 1944, around the age of 25, Lemaire had returned to her hometown to spend Christmas with her parents. Like everyone else, she was eagerly anticipating the end of the war. After the war was over, she planned to wed the local man she had fallen in love with. So that she could sew a bridal dress she would scrounge the silk from Allied parachutes.

After a week filled with deaths, blood, and bandages on Christmas Eve, 1944 a 500-pound German bomb dropped on top of the aid station killing Lemaire and 30 other people. Lemaire had succeeded in rescuing six soldiers from the blazing structure, but he was killed while attempting to save a seventh. She passed away while doing what she was best at... helping.

It took nearly two days before the bodies could be retrieved, at which point they discovered that she had been holding in her hand a piece of white parachute silk. Tragically her future husband would have to wait at the altar... forever. Dr. Prior was able to collect her remains, and returned the body to her parents' home, wrapped in a white silk American parachute. The next day, Allied help arrived, and the siege was lifted, although the neighborhood remained in mourning for several months after her death.

In a request for a post-battle commendation medal made by Battalion Surgeon Dr. Jack T. Prior, Lemaire was described as someone who "cheerfully accepted the Herculean task and worked without adequate rest or food..." that she "changed dressings, fed patients unable to feed themselves, gave out medications, bathed and made the patients more comfortable..." and that "her very presence among those wounded men seem to be an inspiration to those whose morale had declined from prolonged suffering and pain. Many years later, General McAuliffe would make the following observation... "The fact that the Germans were able to seize control of our division hospital was, for me, the single most tragic event of the battle. As a result of my lack of surgeons, I was unable to provide adequate medical attention to the injured. Our injured soldiers were outstanding; I never heard a single complaint from any of them. At one point, I approached the German Commander while flying a white flag and begged him to grant me permission to bring American and German injured in ambulances over the lines to our hospitals. This proposal was turned down," McAuliffe said. "Then on the 26th of December, the allied armored column from the South made contact with the 101st, and they

delivered a large number of ambulances so that all of our injured were then evacuated in a timely manner."

Out of tragedy came hope, mercy and consolation. During the most difficult moments of their lives, these three, Prior, Chiwy and Lemaire gave their all to bring some solace and peace to dying allied soldiers. They were the absolute definition of compassion, and they represented the very best that humanity has to offer. •

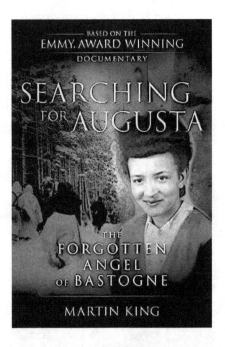

NOTE: Based on the book of the same name, in July 2015 a documentary film about Chiwy, 'Searching for Augusta: The Forgotten Angel of Bastogne' was produced by Martin King and directed by Mike Edwards. It won the Emmy Award for Historical Documentary that year, and is available on Amazon.

CHAPTER 5

War Tools

"We learned the value of research in World War II."
Scientist Amar Bose

First among his passions, McAuliffe enjoyed and excelled at commanding men in battle and fighting with them side-by-side but as his career progressed, more administrative duties were imposed upon him and after a while, he mastered "flying a desk". He most notably supervised and assisted in the development of such exciting and effective new war technologies.

His acceptance to the Army War College, was announced in September of 1939. Upon graduation in June of 1940, he expected to be assigned to an artillery battalion near Salinas, California with a classmate from the War College. However, he was instead assigned to the War Department's General Staff in Washington, DC within G-4, the Logistics Division, the Development Section of the Requirements and Distribution Branch, Supply Division. During his time there McAuliffe was in charge of the Research and Development Department of the Army's complete arsenal, including vehicles and ammunition. His favorite parts of the job were collaborating with scientists and engineers and seeing projects through to completion. The Bazooka, the M-1 Carbine Rifle, Tank-to-Tank radios, the DUKW, a 212-ton

amphibious supply truck, the practically indestructible Army jeep, and the new M-1 helmet were just some of the important military weapons that he worked on during the war. The triumph of the Allies depended on these pieces of equipment, both military and logistical and McAuliffe took pleasure in thinking creatively and collaborating with those who had a background in science to develop strategies that were more efficient at protecting our troops and inflicting maximum harm on the adversary while at the same time minimizing the financial burden on the American tax payer.

•The Bazooka

The 'Bazooka' is a portable recoilless anti-tank rocket launcher weapon that was formerly known as the M1A1 Rocket Launcher and or as the M9.

It gave our soldiers the ability to finally inflict a solid blow to the strongly armored German tanks and fortifications. It was given the moniker "The Stovepipe," and it was equipped with

a solid-propellant rocket for propulsion. Additionally, it could launch a variety of high-explosive anti-tank (HEAT) warheads with an effective range of less than 400 yards. Colonel Leslie Skinner of the United States Army and Lieutenant Edward Uhl of the United States Army began developing the weapon in 1942 at Aberdeen Proving Ground in Maryland. Their efforts were overseen by the United States Army Signal Corps. McAuliffe provided assistance and participated in the project's management.

During the course of the war, the Bazooka was considered to be one of the most effective "tank killers." Our troops were able to remove the tracks off German tanks by using bazookas as their primary weapon. McAuliffe stated. "You see, it was heavily wooded there (in the Ardennes forest), and our guys would just let the tank go by on the road and then they'd step out of the woods, and with the Bazooka they couldn't penetrate these tanks because they were too thick, but they could knock the tracks off, and that would immobilize the tanks," said McAuliffe.

Later, General Dwight Eisenhower referred to the Bazooka as one of the four essential "*Tools of Victory*" that helped the Allies win the war (the other

three were the atomic bomb, the Jeep, and the C-47 Skytrain Transport Aircraft).

•**DUKW** *(Amphibious Landing Vehicle, "The Duck")* Many historians believe that the Allied D-Day landing on the beaches of Normandy would not have been as successful or even conceivable if it had not been for the use of 'The Duck.' Following the D-Day invasion on June 6, 1944, DUKWs moved more than 10 million pounds of supplies in the first 30 days after the invasion alone!

It was necessary to devise a plan to get massive amounts of supplies from the ships, down the coastline, and inland to the troops, but at the time, there was nothing that could be done to accomplish this. However, by the time of D-Day, there was! The amphibious vehicle known as the DUKW, which he had a hand in developing and McAuliffe is quoted as saying, "We'd never have gotten the supplies ashore at Normandy if we hadn't had the Duck! (DUKW). We entertained the idea of making landfall in Europe, specifically on the coast of France, but it was never really clear to us how we were going to bring in food and other necessities once we did so. I was aware with all of the vehicles that were available, including a track vehicle known as the 'Roebling Alligator' that had been utilized well by the Navy in the Pacific theater of operations "he stated. "It has use both in the sea and on dry ground. However, after looking into the manufacturing possibilities, I came to the conclusion that it would be impossible to make it in the quantities that would be necessary." And the Allies would want a large quantity of them to be sure.

"On D-Day, after I parachuted into Normandy, I remember standing up on that hill overlooking the Beaches and watching all those colored soldiers (of the 'Cannonball Express') move those supplies, which weighed thousands of tons in total, from the ships into, over, and up the beaches to waiting troops. It was a performance of the highest caliber, and I have no idea how we could have accomplished it any other way. The Germans had mined the harbor at Cherbourg so thoroughly with these underwater "timed mines" that would surface three to four weeks after we had seized the town. As a result, we were unable to utilize that harbor until around six weeks after it was all over. But we were required to keep supplying the whole Army stationed on the

Cherbourg Peninsula via these DUKWs as they traveled from ship to beach over and over again non-stop, 24/7."

•The Jeep

Because of its reputation for being nearly impossible to wreck, the Jeep quickly rose to prominence as the most important method of transportation throughout the war. It could be used as an attack platform with an M-60 machine gun attached to the back, it could be utilized as a medical ambulance, and it could be used for general military transportation. The Jeep had two important advantages: it required little maintenance, and it was fuel-efficient. Both of these advantages were important to the military. The team led by McAuliffe collaborated with automotive manufacturers to enhance the Jeep's fuel efficiency, suspension, and its dependability.

• The Carbine Rifle Model 1 (M1)

The M1 is a lightweight semi-automatic carbine that served as a standard weapon for the United States

military throughout World War II, the Korean War, and the Vietnam War. It was designated as the "M1 Carbine." The weapon with a caliber of.30 has an effective range of 300 yards and was in service between the years 1943 and 1973. It is still utilized to a significant degree by a variety of paramilitary and police groups all around the world. During World War II, the United States military produced more than 6.1 million different types of the M1 carbine, making it the most widely produced kind of infantry weapon in that country. In general, the M-16 and the M4 have taken its position as the standard issue weapon.

•**Tank-to-Tank Radio**, (or T2R for short).
The inability of tank commanders to efficiently and wirelessly communicate with one another while they were out in the field was one of the issues that arose early on during the Tanks conflict. Through the collaboration of MIT and Motorola Corporation, a wireless tank-to-tank radio was developed; the initial range of the device was restricted, but it has since been expanded.

•**The M1 Helmet**
The M1 combat helmet was used by members of the United States armed forces from the time of World War II until the year 1985. The M1 helmet was the norm for a number of decades. More than 22 million of them were produced specifically for World War Two. It was in service from 1941 until 1985. The outer shell of the M1 helmet was constructed of manganese steel and was rather heavy. The helmet

was not designed to withstand the impact of a bullet. Rather, the focus was on protecting the soldier from any impacts to the head as well as fragments, shrapnel, and explosive debris that may be flying around during the firefight. At the beginning of the war, McAuliffe's team contributed to the design of a better, more ventilation-friendly harness that attached the helmet to the head. They also contributed to the design of netting that dimmed the shine of the helmet, which was more than just an annoyance out in the field, and the netting allowed

for the storage of small items on the exterior of the helmet. During both the Korean War and the Vietnam War, research and development efforts were maintained. As a result, in 1985, the military began issuing the new PASGT helmet, which had improved ergonomics, reduced weight, and enhanced protection against ballistics.

Building on his successes McAuliffe was promoted to the position of Chief of the Ordnance and Coast Artillery Section under the Development Branch of the Supply Division in January of 1942. As a direct result of his work on this mission, he was given the rank of full Colonel on February 1, 1942.

McAuliffe's first job at the R&D desk was to compose a letter of response to a memorandum that had been sent by the Prime Minister of the United Kingdom, Winston Churchill, to the President of the United States, Franklin D. Roosevelt. Even though the United States was not yet a combatant in the war at that time, in 1940, it was supplying Great Britain with military hardware. Prime Minister Churchill suggested seven improvements to be made to the firearms used and manufactured by the United States. The President gave the memorandum to General George Marshall, who was the Chief of Staff for the Army. General Marshall, in turn, gave it to Lieutenant Colonel Henry Aurand, who was the head of the Requirements and Distribution Branch. Lieutenant Colonel Henry Aurand, in turn, gave it to McAuliffe

The number of charges for the 105mm howitzer was to be reduced from seven to three, the 37mm anti-aircraft gun was to be abandoned and replaced with the Bofors 40mm, production of the Boys.55 caliber anti-tank rifle was to begin, and the British 3.7 inch gun was to be adopted as the high-altitude anti-aircraft gun. These were just some of the changes that were proposed. Tony stated that he had originally missed many nights' sleep due to his anxiety over this task because it involved Winston Churchill, President Roosevelt, and General Marshall, but he was just a Captain at the time. Tony sought the advice of a number of his classmates from the War College who were also working for the Department of Defense and who possessed a better understanding of the ordnance components as well as the political landscape.

After much deliberation, he chose to eventually shrug it off and hand in his recommendations. In response to Mr. Churchill's memorandum, he recommended turning down all of the suggestions with the exception of one. He suggested switching to the Bofors 40mm anti-aircraft gun and discontinuing production of the 37mm anti-aircraft gun. In front of a number of Generals, he was required to argue the merits of his proposals with the Chief of Ordnance at the time, Major General Charles "Bull" Wesson. Tony's suggestion to replace the 37mm gun was met with opposition and disagreement by General Wesson, who argued against the idea. Tony's suggestions were ultimately approved by General Marshall, which led to the selection of the Bofors 40mm anti-aircraft gun as the weapon of choice. Wesson was so upset with General McAuliffe that he never spoke to him again!

On another occasion, Tony was forced to stop production of a new medium Tank because it had not gone through the appropriate development sequence. In order for him to be successful doing this, he recruited the assistance of General Jacob Devers, who was the Commander of the Armored Forces. Tony received assistance from General

Devers in the process of creating the amphibious DUKW vehicle. Throughout all of Tony's time spent in the Army, his friendship with General Devers remained strong. McAuliffe learned to appreciate the fact that he could contribute to the war effort without being front and center. But it was abundantly clear that even though McAuliffe missed commanding men in battle, which the author believes was his first best destiny, he came to realize that there were many other ways for him to contribute his many special talents to the war effort.

It was abundantly clear that McAuliffe could significantly contribute in other ways. During this period, two other things also became abundantly clear to everyone: the first was that solider Tony McAuliffe was not afraid to argue with his superiors if he believed he was in the right, and the second was that he was able to think creatively and surround himself with individuals who could do the same. In later years, McAuliffe was instrumental in bringing the United States into the atomic era. Because of the bomb, everything changed, and he saw that straight away... it rendered traditional combat obsolete. As with many other things that occurred throughout his long career, McAuliffe found himself on the precipice of history... again.

He went on to the Pacific theater to help test the first atomic bombs. "Those were the first nuclear bomb tests ever conducted and it was huge in more ways than one!" he added with a grin. According to McAuliffe, "All of the newspaper front pages were

filled with images of both the air and water bursts and with comments from everyone interested, scientists, the military, mothers, politicians, and everyone else," he said. "I was a little concerned that my involvement with the atomic bomb might make me eligible for that kind of duty. So as soon as I was able to, I jumped back into the old rat race of inventing tanks, rifles, and other standard military stuff...everything else that the American soldier utilizes to fight." McAuliffe came to the conclusion that if he could no longer command troops in battle, the next best thing would be to ensure that those troops had the dependable and cutting-edge equipment they needed for victory. •

CHAPTER 6

C-h-a-n-g-e

"I know not with what weapons World War III will be fought, but World War IV will be fought with sticks and stones."
Albert Einstein.

Immediately following the war, McAuliffe served in a variety of commands including as Chief of the United States Army Chemical Corps and as 'G-1,' Head of Army Personnel. As the military morphed from a war footing to a peacetime cadence, there was always a lot of personnel shifting and command changes. McAuliffe recalled that it was the same after World War I. After serving as Commander of the Seventh Army upon his return to Europe in 1953, he was promoted to the position of Commander-in-Chief of the United States Army Europe the following year. In 1955, he was one of a select few to be awarded the rank of four-star general. In the 245-year history of the US Army there have been 251 Four-Star Generals but only five officers that have reached the rank of 5.

The 1950s were at hand and the world was undergoing enormous and fundamental changes. One of the main areas that was being affected was the state of racial relations in the United States. And just as with many other aspects of General McAuliffe's life and career, he was again on the cutting edge of history and fully involved in these momentous events. McAuliffe was at the forefront of this difficult transformation and the Army was one of the first military services and federal government organizations to attempt complete integration between the races. The transition to a colorblind Army was to be one of the most fundamental and dramatic events in the history of the United States Army. The crime of racism was to be eradicated from the ranks.

"A number of recommendations about the full incorporation of Negros into the ranks were delivered by the War College to the War Department, where they were reviewed, approved, and implemented by the General Staff. After much consideration, I came to the conclusion that we needed to integrate, and the sooner, the better," McAuliffe said. "Well, we did. And by the time we integrated, I was serving in the role of G-1 Assistant Chief of Staff, which gave me oversight over personnel matters. I was a Lieutenant General at the time, and it was somewhere about 1950; we began our journey towards equality in Camp Jackson, South Carolina, of all places!

After completing the integration of the training commands, we moved on to our mission in Korea. McAuliffe said that the battle was still going on over there, and that we had some difficulties with the African-American unit that was serving with the 24th Infantry of the 25th Division. "The National Association for the Advancement of Colored People (NAACP) and other African American groups were, without a doubt, advocating for integration. The Army Chief of Staff , myself, and the Secretary of Defense all believed in integration. So, we began our journey, if you will, in Korea, and then moved on to Camp Jackson in South Carolina. They weren't going to have an easy time integrating back into society in the United States, but it was evident that if they merged in Korea, they had to integrate here once the troops came back. Also, if you merged here, you had to integrate with the occupying troops in Europe as well," he explained. "In Europe, the Commander there, who was from the South, didn't want any part of integration and objected vehemently against it. There was also a lot of resistance by some of the top Generals, but we were able to overcome it. The social aspect was the primary issue. It was the snack bar, the swimming pool, and the dances that caused you issues, therefore avoid those areas at all costs," he added. "Whites and colored people fought together, tented together, ate together, and did everything else together during World War II. Our level of integration had already reached a significant level prior to the end of the war. It was therefore, not a novel experience for many of the more experienced soldiers. President Truman was therefore extremely delighted that we were able to accomplish this goal," McAuliffe remarked. "Now, I've heard that Truman with Presidential Order 9981 is attributed with having instructed the Army to integrate, but having been there, I can say with certainty that this was not the case. Despite his extreme pleasure, he did not make the order." To him, it was not complicated...

Integration and equality meant higher levels of operational effectiveness and military readiness, which was exactly what he wanted to see. McAuliffe believed that honor and duty knows no color.

After the siege of Bastogne, General McAuliffe commanded the 103rd Infantry Division in its rapid drive southward through Germany and Austria to make a junction with elements of the American Fifth Army at Vipiteno, Italy. This resulted in the 19th German Army being forced to unconditionally surrender. His superiors, from Ike on down believed, and stated on multiple occasions, that it was McAuliffe's extraordinary military skill, innovative thought, constant aggressiveness, and complete devotion to duty that contributed materially to bringing the war in Europe to a swift and successful conclusion. Perhaps the best way to sum it all was when McAuliffe was presented with the Army Meritorious Service Medal upon his retirement from active duty in 1956. They said....

"General McAuliffe distinguished himself by providing exceptionally meritorious service while serving as Commanding General, Seventh Army, and later as Commander-in-Chief, United States Army Europe, between the dates of 20 October 1953 and 30 April 1956. During this time, he was in a position of great trust and responsibility. His multifaceted forces were able to attain and keep an extremely high level of combat preparedness because to his superb leadership and forceful direction. The ever-evolving state of world affairs

necessitated that General McAuliffe successfully invent new methods of battle. He was successful in meeting these needs. When it came to the planning and directing of the actions of this crucial command, his extensive expertise as well as his awareness of the diplomatic and political ramifications played an extremely important role. His exceptional leadership and remarkable professional expertise served as a source of motivation for everyone who had the opportunity to work with him. The unshakable allegiance and honesty of General McAuliffe, as well as his unrivaled position among his troops, reflect the ultimate honor upon both himself and the military service as a whole." Amen!

America was indeed fortunate to have such a good Stewart to help steer its defense. "I think most of the good decisions I made during World War II were dictated by the principles that were so thoroughly beaten into me during that year at the US Army's Command and General Staff School," he recalled. "To clear things up, though, strategy was never really an issue for me in my professional life. It was all a matter of tactics." McAulife went where they sent him and may not have been very involved in establishing strategy but one cannot argue the results via his tactics. They say when one door closes another one opens and as the 1960s came on McAuliffe had more to give and was not yet ready to retire. •

CHAPTER 7

Puttin' on Civies

"A veteran who comes home from war is returning from one of the most intense experiences a human being can have. Even if he was not under fire every day...He started every day with a purpose, and a mission that mattered to those around him."
Eric Greitens

In 1956 McAuliffe retired from Army Active Duty and the only life he had ever known. He was eligible for early retirement under a law that allowed officers who had served in both World Wars to do so. He only served for ten days during World War I, but it was just long enough to make him eligible. On June 1, 1956, he officially retired and was given credit for 37 years and 7 months of Active Duty military service.

He didn't waste any time transitioning to civilian life and accepted a key post with Cyanamid Corporation, which was one of the top chemical companies in America at the time. He worked there from 1956 till 1963. As Vice President for Personnel, he was responsible for a number of successes, one of which was the creation of an innovative program that teaches workers of the firm how to maintain touch and positive ties with local political groups and other governmental bodies. After that, the corporation made it mandatory for all of the Branch Managers to make at least a brief introduction to local lawmakers. He then became Vice President for Engineering and Construction, a job which had not existed prior to then and a few years later was General Manager.

During his post-Army years, McAuliffe also served on the Board of Directors of a number of different businesses and civic organizations. Perhaps the most

major was his role as Chairman of the New York State Civil Defense Commission from 1960 to 1963. But after his time on active duty, he may have been connected with the United States Military Academy

(West Point) more than any other group. In 1957, he was given a position as a Trustee on the Board of Visitors for a tenure that would last for three years. However, after serving as a trustee, he was ultimately successful in running for the presidency of the Association of Graduates. He was elected to three terms that each lasted a year. After finishing he was chosen to serve on the Board of Trustees once more. In 1965, he was bestowed the title of 'Honorary Trustee for Life'. After being honored as one of the Military Academy's twenty-seven 'Illustrious Graduates' at a banquet held in New York City in 1967, he went on to become President of the Military Academy's 'Association of Graduates'.

Although perhaps not his favorite pastime McAuliffe was an accomplished public speaker. In February of 1963, he was the keynote speaker at an event that marked the dedication of the Selby Chemistry Building at Marietta College in Ohio. After the ceremony, the university bestowed upon him an honorary degree with the title "Doctor of Laws." That accolade was never spoken of outside of his family, and the other members of his family didn't discover the documents on it until a significant amount of time had elapsed after he had passed away. And that was just his self-effacing way... Tony McAuliffe never bragged about his achievements; he let his work speak for itself... and it does even after 75 years.

Tony continued to be involved after his retirement by serving others in a variety of capacities and organizations, including the 101st Airborne Association, the Army Distaff Foundation, the Army- Navy Club, the Military Order of the World Wars, the Veterans of Foreign Wars, and the

American Legion. In addition to that, he was a member of the board of directors for a number of civic groups, including the Washington National Ballet and American Red Cross.

Tony passed away from Leukemia. on August 10, 1975 at the Walter Reed Army Medical Center. He was 77 years old. He's buried at Arlington National

Cemetery, in Virginia and is laid to rest with his family. The honors that were bestowed upon this soldier for his service remain forever.

The accolades are far too numerous to list all of them here, but some of the highlights include; The central square of Bastogne, Belgium, is named 'Place Général McAuliffe' or 'McAuliffe Square.' and a bust of General McAuliffe with a Sherman tank that has been pierced by a German 88 mm shell is on display. There are other monuments. For example in the United States of America... 'General Anthony Clement McAuliffe 101st Airborne Memorial Highway' is the name given to Route 33 in eastern Pennsylvania. Elsewhere the new headquarters building for the United States Army's 101st Airborne Division at Fort Campbell, Kentucky, has been given the name "McAuliffe Hall," and a room at the Thayer Hotel near West Point (that the author has stayed in) has been named "The McAuliffe Suite" in honor of the General. There are many other honors.

Over the course of his life, General Tony McAuliffe has been recognized for his achievements in the military with more than twenty-five major military medals and decorations. In addition, there have been many coins and stamps released by a variety of nations to celebrate his service and accomplishments. However, this author is of the opinion that if the General were still living today, he would consider his most significant achievement to be the fact that he was able to bring up three wonderful children and have a happy married life with his wife Helen for more than 40 years.

He was a comfortable solider bureaucrat and could have easily sat out the war in safety behind a desk in the Pentagon but instead he gave it all up to get in the fight against fascism and make a difference. One thing is certain... sadly we shall not see the likes of him ever again! •

CHAPTER 8

The Tally

"War is a racket. It is the only one international in scope. It is the only one in which the profits are reckoned in dollars and the losses in lives."
General Smedley Butler, USMC

To fully put General Tony McAuliffe's lifetime of service in context and perspective it is important to examine the full scope of what occurred during his career. He was in a unique position to observe history having served, however briefly, in the era of World War I, where the army was still using Horses and Cannon until World War II and the Korean War with the invention of modern jet aircraft and nuclear weapons... all on his watch.

The second world war happened between 1939 and 1945. It is believed that between 70 and 85 million people died, which is roughly 3 percent of the approximately 2.3 billion people who were living on Earth at the time. It is believed that between 50 and 56 million people lost their lives as a direct result of the conflict, including both military and civilian casualties. It is also estimated that between 19 and 28 million people lost their lives as a direct result of the war-related diseases, starvation, and disasters. Despite the fact that only 2 million of the more than 16 million Americans who served in the war did so in Europe, the conflict against the Nazi's occupies a very disproportionate amount of space in the

American psyche. But it is incredible how many people from the USA had enlisted, since there were around 140 million people living in America in 1945, this means that an amazing 11.3% of all Americans served.

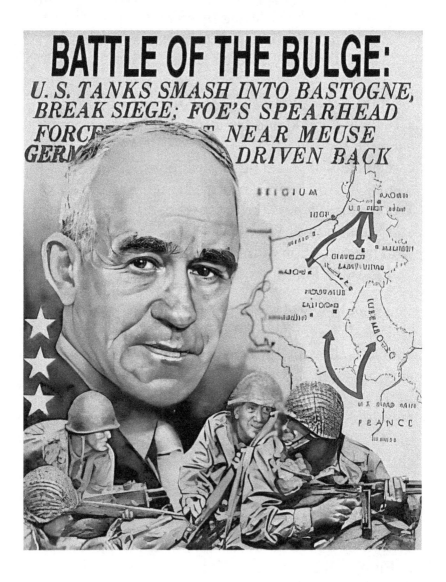

Those who served are an aging population. It's estimated that overall today's veterans are 65 years old on average. Veterans who served after September 11, 2001 have a median age of around 37 years old, soldiers who served during Vietnam have a median age of approximately 71 years old, and veterans who served during World War II have a median age of approximately 93 years old.

It's believed that nearly one million Allied forces participated in the Battle of the Bulge, including 500,000 soldiers from the United States of America. On the battlefield, around 19,000 American soldiers were killed, while another 47,500 were injured and 23,000 were reported missing in action.

Here are some other fascinating facts and figures:

Total Deaths in Battle = Approximately 15 million
Wounded = 25,000,000
Civilian deaths = 45,000,000
Refugees = 16,000,000
US Battle of the Bulge Deaths = 80,000
US troops dead in World War II= 405,399
German Military Deaths = Approx. 5.5 million
Russian Deaths = Estimated at 20 million
Japan Deaths= Estimated at 2.6 million
Aircraft Produced = 916k
Tanks = 280k
Artillery = 257,400
Warships = 1410
194 countries participated
Total deaths: Approx. 60 to 70,000,000

HEADQUARTERS 101ST AIRBORNE DIVISION
Office of the Division Commander

24 December 1944

What's Merry about all this, you ask? We're fighting - it's cold we aren't home. All true but what has the proud Eagle Division accomplished with its worthy comrades of the 10th Armored Division, the 705th Tank Destroyer Battalion and all the rest? Just this: We have stopped cold everything that has been thrown at us from the North, East, South and West. We have identifications from four German Panzer Divisions, two German Infantry Divisions and one German Parachute Division. These units, spearheading the last desperate German lunge, were headed straight west for key points when the Eagle Division was hurriedly ordered to stem the advance. How effectively this was done will be written in history; not alone in our Division's glorious history but in World history. The Germans actually did surround us their radios blared our doom. Their Commander demanded our surrender in the following impudent arrogance.

December 22nd 1944

"To the U. S. A. Commander of the encircled town of Bastogne.

The fortune of war is changing. This time the U. S. A. forces in and near Bastogne have been encircled by strong German armored units. More German armored units have crossed the river Ourthe near Ortheuville, have taken Marche and reached St. Hubert by passing through Hombres-Sibret-Tillet. Libramont is in German hands.

There is only one possibility to save the encircled U. S. A. Troop from total annihilation: that is the honorable surrender of the encircled town. In order to think it over a term of two hours will be granted beginning with the presentation of this note.

If this proposal should be rejected one German Artillery Corps and six heavy A. A. Battalions are ready to annihilate the U. S. A. Troops in and near Bastogne. The order for firing will be given immediately after this two hour's term.

All the serious civilian losses caused by this artillery fire would not correspond with the well known American humanity.

The German Commander

The German Commander received the following reply:

22 December 1944

To the German Commander:

N U T S !

The American Commander

Allied Troops are counterattacking in force. We continue to hold Bastogne. By holding Bastogne we assure the success of the Allied armies. We know that our Division Commander, General Taylor, will say: "Well Done!"

We are giving our country and our loved ones at home a worthy Christmas present and being privileged to take part in this gallant feat of arms are truly making for ourselves a Merry Christmas.

McAULIFFE
Commanding

Christmas Newsletter, Bastogne, 1944

Total Cost of the War: $125-150 trillion
Marshall Plan to rebuild Europe = $12 billion
From National World War Two Museum

• Over 1,000,000 miles were marched during the Battle of the Bulge alone.

• Next to Normandy in France, Bastogne in Belgium is the most visited World War II battle site.

• There were only 20 major battles in Europe

• Soldiers had a toilet paper ration of 22 sheets a day

• General McAuliffe was an avid card player, an excellent Dancer and also followed Thoroughbred Horse Racing closely.

• During the war burgers were called "Liberty Steaks" because the word "hamburger" sounded to German.

• During the siege at Bastogne it was the coldest winner in 103 years with the longest period of subzero temperatures. The record remains unbroken.

• The December 23 re-supply was one of the largest air drops of the war with a record 240 planes dropping more than 1400 bundles of supplies into a one square mile area.

• A 1921 West Point graduate, McAuliffe was 29th in a class of 284.

• Hundreds of limbs were lost due to frostbite during the Battle of the Bulge.

• It's estimated that had the German Tanks had another 100,000 liters of fuel they may have achieved their goal of the port of Antwerp.

• During the siege America soldiers were down to a few bullets each.

Bastogne Belgium Order of Battle
(before 26 December 1944)

101st Airborne Division

CCB of the 10th Armored Division

CCR of the 9th Armored Division

705th and 510th Tank Destroyer Battalions

35th and 158th Combat Engineer Battalions

58th and 420th Armored Field Artillery Battalions

755th & 969th Field Artillery Battalions of 8th Corps

Team SNAFU [remnants of 28th ID unit]

(None of these units were at full strength.)

General Tony C. McAuliffe
<u>Medals & Citations</u>

Army Distinguished Service Cross
Army Distinguished Service-Oak Leaf Cluster
The Silver Star
The Legion of Merit
Bronze Star with V for Valor
Victory Medal, World War I with Oak Leaf Cluster
Army of Occupation Medal-Germany with 4 stars
Victory Medal, World War II
Army of Occupation Medal, World War II
Germany Service Medal
Japan Service Medal
National Defense Service Medal
Presidential Unit Citation with Oak Leaf Cluster
US Army Parachutist emblem with three stars
US Army Airborne Glider Badge
British Distinguished Service Order with Bar
French Legion of Honor
French Croix de Guerre with Palm
Netherlands Order of the Bronze Lion
Belgian Order of Leopold
Luxembourg Order of the Oak Crown
Netherlands Orange Lanyard
Belgian Fourragere of 1940

GENERAL ANTHONY McAULIFFE
USMA 1918

"NUTS!"

COMMANDER OF DIVISION ARTILLERY 101ST AIRBORNE ON D-DAY

TING COMMANDER 101ST DIVISION AIRBORNE SIEGE OF BASTOG

IN RESPONSE TO GERMAN REQUEST OF SURRENDER REPLIED:
THE GERMAN COMMANDER, NUTS!, THE AMERICAN COMMANDE

COMMANDER 103D INFANTRY DIVISION - WWII

COMMANDER-IN-CHIEF UNITED STATES ARMY EUROPE

DUTY ★ HONOR ★ COUNTRY

CHAPTER 9

The Quotes of General McAuliffe

"If there's any lesson to be learned from Bastogne, I guess it's the same sort of lesson that might be learned from the Battle of Midway. That critical battle where the Japanese Naval carrier task force was destroyed from the air or the bombing of Japan under General Dolittle. The lesson to me is that those battles gave the lie to those who said that in this country, we had gone soft that this country like the Roman empire was on its way to disintegration, to a weakness caused by prosperity and good living. Those battles proved that those rugged pioneer virtues that moved our forefathers to found this great country still live in the hearts and the minds of young Americans, their lives, our strength today, their lives, our military strength, not anatomic bombs, not in guided missiles, but in the courage, the initiative, the resort of the American people, as long as we cultivate, maintain those high qualities and talents so long, shall we have no fear? The atomic bomb, the supersonic airplane, the great industries are billions of skilled workmen. Our only outward evidences of that inner strength. My secret weapon at Bastogne was the spirit of my troops. The secret weapon for the defense of the United States is the spirit of our people. It has been the basis of all our past triumphs. For me, it is our greatest hope today for the future."
Speech, Detroit 1956

"We resented the implication that we were rescued. We never needed rescue! I was never forced to use a Division reserve and our situation was never truly desperate, at least in our eyes."
Bastogne 50th Anniversary ceremonies

"If you talk to the former Mayor of Bastogne, who was there at the battle, he'll tell you without bitterness, really how the Americans stole his prized typewriter and drank up all his best wine!"
Bastogne 50th Anniversary ceremonies

These quotes are taken from an interview with General McAuliffe at Columbia University in 1963:

"Our morale was terrific. When you're traveling 50 or 60 miles a day through enemy territory, gee – I didn't even let them sleep. These tanks would stop and there'd be 40 GIs on there and they'd all fall asleep or get off on the side of the road and fall asleep, sleep for 20 minutes, and have to get back on. Nobody slept. When you're pursuing – this is another Command and General Staff School thing – you never let up on the troops; you just drive them every inch of the way because this is where you really make money: where you capture many enemy and suffer very few casualties yourself. So, I really drove them, and they loved it. And they loved Innsbruck. I moved them all into these resort hotels and they didn't even make their own beds. I started the brewery going, making beer. They lived in

beautiful resort hotels, and with all the staffs practically there. We really had it good!"

"The SS Troops fought and fought hard, and our people killed the S.S. Commander, a Major, and one of the things they found on him was a bag of gold fillings from the teeth of concentration camp victims."

"I thought Patton was a great fellow and a great Army Commander. I have the idea that in that kind of war, in modern war, to command as many troops as Patton commanded you have to be an actor and you have to dramatize yourself to be successful, and I point to Patton and Montgomery as two such colorful personalities. They were adored by their troops. I knew Patton well. I'd played polo with him in Hawaii. I'd know him for years. And most of us thought he never had a very good staff but he certainly accomplished miracles with it. I think his campaign in Sicily will go down in history as one of the great ones. And this business of turning that Army of his around to drive north to relieve us at Bastonge, the way he went about that was remarkable too. I mean the success of moving an unwieldy mass like that, to change your lines of supply, and everything, to turn that cumbersome heavy-going outfit in the snow, in the fog, and the rain, and turn them to the north, was really a remarkable task to accomplish."

"So, I went to General Patton and told him that I'd like to get command of a division that was going to the Pacific. He told me I was a damned fool to take on any such thing and that I'd get a bad deal from MacArthur, and I said, "I'd like to go anyway". "Okay," he said, "I'll get you a command.""

"She took it like a soldier. Army wives are better soldiers than the men!"

"I didn't like Pentagon duty. It's frustrating, and you've got a lot of civilians looking over your shoulder with no authority, except to question and argue and criticize."

"We've had lots of wars since World War II, but massive retaliation has never been the answer to any of them."

"I don't think people join the Army or the Navy or the Air Force for the money. I've never regretted my military career. It was very satisfying. I think there are other things that are more important than money, and still are. But when you get around 60 years old, or 55, and you have children, you get more concerned about leaving them so that they will be able to live decently and well, and money becomes, I think, a more important factor as you get older."

"I wasn't one of these fellows who wanted an office in the Pentagon with windows opening with two views toward different areas. I never bothered much with that. I always lived pretty simply and frugally."

"It always seems when you get a broken femur or something like that, that the man is the one key fellow you're counting on for combat operations!"

//////

Acknowledgments

Kenneth J. McAuliffe, Jr.

The Estate of General Anthony McAuliffe

The United States Army PAO, Wash. DC

101st Airborne Public Affairs, Ft. Campbell, KY

The City of Bastogne, Belgium

United States Library of Congress

WWII Museum, New Orleans, LA

The WWII Veterans Project

American Veterans Center

Advisor Dale L. Roberts

Advisor Brian Meeks

*Veterans from all wars who have stepped
forward to defend our nation!*

Other Books by Author Tom McAuliffe

THE 'McAuliffe' SERIES

• **Mr. Mulligan** - *The Life of Champion Armless Golfer Tommy McAuliffe*

• **Nuts!** - *The Life & Times of General Tony McAuliffe*

• **Throttle up** - Astronaut & Teacher Christa McAuliffe

• **Mad Dog!** - *1968 World Series Champ & Detroit Tiger Dick McAuliffe*

• **Life of the Party** - *Governor Terry McAuliffe*

On sale at Amazon, Kindle, Apple iBooks, Barnes & Noble and your favorite local independent book store.

PLEASE LEAVE US A REVIEW!

Please visit:
WWW.AUTHORTOMMCAULIFFE.COM

www.ingramcontent.com/pod-product-compliance
Lightning Source LLC
La Vergne TN
LVHW092008280325
807154LV00008B/113